Golden Moments

by Grace Noll Crowell

"Where can one find poetry?" one asks.
Not alone in moonlight, blossoms, birds, and trees,
But in the articles used in our daily tasks:
The homely things of living such as these—
A plow whose share has cleaved the stubborn soil,
A churn, a mixing bowl in women's hands,
A scythe, a hoe—mute emblems of men's toil,
The things of constant usage in all lands.

They hold within their depths a song that sings,
And still will sing as long as earth shall last:
Old, elemental, fundamental things
Essential to the present and the past,
Not beautiful in their austerity,
But meaning much—are steeped in poetry.

ACKNOWLEDGMENTS

CHRISTMAS TODAY and PRAYER FOR THE NEW
YEAR, Courtesy *The Dallas Morning News.* HOSPITAL-
ITY; LABOR THAT REPAYS; LAST SNOW; PITY,
previously published in *Successful Farming.* Courtesy
Meredith Corporation. FARM-BORN; HOME; HOME-
ABIDING WOMEN; THE HORSES; POETRY, Copyright
by The Progressive Farmer Co., reprinted from *Progressive
Farmer* Magazine. CORDWOOD; THE FEEL OF AU-
TUMN; SOON WILL THE FLUTED POOLS, previously
published in *The Washington Star,* Washington D.C.

ISBN 0-89542-075-9 395

Published by Ideals Publishing Corporation
11315 Watertown Plank Road
Milwaukee, Wisconsin 53226

Editorial Director, James Kuse
Managing Editor, Ralph Luedtke
Production Editor/Manager, Richard Lawson
Photographic Editor, Gerald Koser
Copy Editor, Sharon Style

Designed by Beverly Rae Wiersum

Grace Noll Crowell

A little girl, with long brown braids flying in the wind, races across the meadow. Skirting the newly plowed field, she snatches an apple from a tree in the orchard and collapses breathlessly under the shade of an ancient oak tree. Munching the juicy, sun-ripened fruit, she leans against the sturdy trunk, gazes up at the translucent clouds, and dreams about life. Through her girlish imagination she sees herself as a singer, an artist, a queen, or one of the glamorous women she has read about. Finally, with characteristic realism, she returns to the reality of a woman's role in turn-of-the-century America—that of wife and mother—and looks forward to that life with excitement and enthusiasm. Little does young Grace Noll Crowell realize all that life holds in store for her.

In all her visions of the future, not once did young Grace Gabrielle Noll envision herself as the successful and world-famous poet she was to become. Although she always longed to write poetry, she considered her first poem so disappointing that she was discouraged from future writing. She turned instead to the satisfying challenges of caring for a house, husband, and children and reading poetry in her spare time.

Miss Noll found little spare time in her early life. In 1901, at the age of twenty-four she left her home and parents in Inland, Iowa, and married a promising young newspaper man, Norman H. Crowell, from Dallas, Texas. The duties of a housewife kept her cheerfully busy, turning their house into a home. A few years later, she found herself spending most of her time fashioning baby clothes out of leftover material as she anxiously awaited the arrival of their first child.

The excitement and joy of giving birth to a son, however, were overshadowed by sadness, for it was discovered that Mrs. Crowell had developed a spinal disorder and nervous weakness. Confined to her bed for long and tedious hours, Mrs. Crowell patiently bore her pain in silence. Because she was unable to go about her household duties as before, she determined to write once again. Recalling her try at poetry, she said, "One day I took pen and paper and wrote a little verse. Its poor feet faltered and stumbled, but at least they got somewhere. And, suddenly, I was filled with an intense longing to write!" She was halfway there; she had the desire and the inspiration but still needed the confidence.

Mrs. Crowell believed her lack of practical training in writing left her at a disadvantage, and she turned to God for assistance. "I came humbly to the Lord and put my case before him. I told him I just couldn't bear to be so useless, and if he would let me write poetry, I would always try to honor him with my pen. That never would I write a thing whose sentiment I would be ashamed to have him see.

I kept my part, and he marvelously seems to have been interested enough to have entered into a compact." Despite her recurring illness, the bargain was maintained.

As she gained confidence in her writing, each poem came more easily than the preceding one. After several poems were written, her husband Norman realized the seriousness of her endeavor and sent a poem to *Outing Magazine*. To their surprise, the editor accepted and published it. This poem, "The Marshland," was the beginning of a long and prolific career which resulted in the publication of nearly 5,000 poems, twenty-two books of poetry, seven devotional prose books, and eight children's books.

Critics attribute the instant and widespread success of Mrs. Crowell's poetry to her empathy with others, a result perhaps of her frequent bouts with illness. During these times, Mrs. Crowell became well acquainted with pain and suffering, fear and doubt. Rather than succumb to bitterness, however, she opened her heart to unselfish and loving compassion; and her deep-rooted faith in God enabled her to help others who suffered, either from physical pain, mental anguish, or spiritual need. "Most of my verse was written as I lay here in the bed and waited for the time when I could walk again. I guess they come to me better at those times." Through her poetry, she encouraged her readers to find hope and comfort by looking beyond themselves and their individual situations to the simple beauty of daily living. Drawing upon happy childhood memories of her Iowa homestead, she celebrated the common by infusing her poetry with vivid rural imagery.

Throughout her lifetime, Mrs. Crowell won many awards and honors for her poetry, including the National Poetry Center's selection as Honor Poet of Poetry Week in 1938. She also served as Poet Laureate of Texas from 1935 to 1939 and received an honorary degree of Doctor of Literature from Baylor University. More importantly to Mrs. Crowell, her poetry enabled her to touch the hearts of millions who needed the courage, faith, and inspiration to help themselves. In fact, when asked how she would like to be known in the literary world, she replied, "as a lyric and religious poet who has helped her fellowman."

With all her success, however, Mrs. Crowell never neglected her husband and three sons. Her role as wife and mother always held precedence over her position as an internationally acclaimed poet. In spite of her illness, she continued taking care of her home and family; and in 1938 the Golden Rule Foundation selected her as American Mother of the Year. In her typically modest way, she felt she deserved the award no more than any other mother.

Grace Noll Crowell died in 1969, sixteen years after her husband, but she still touches the hearts of those who read her poetry. Through her faith, hope, and optimism, everyone can, like Mrs. Crowell, discover the gold in each moment.

Farm-born

I am a part of that furrow,
I am a part of the seed
Sown in the long-still darkness
To meet a hunger need.

        I am one with the wheat field,
        I am one with the corn,
        I am a farmer's daughter,
        And the land where I was born

Is part of my blood and sinew,
Is part of my nerve and brain,
The sun above white acres,
The wind, the lashing rain

        Are my heritage, my birthright,
        And all that I have known
        Of wealth lie in those riches
        Peculiarly my own.

Home-abiding Women

The home-abiding women of all lands
Who love and serve within their quiet places
With light, swift-moving feet and busy hands,
The beauty of contentment on their faces—
These women, who wait long, who trust and pray,
Help steady this old earth upon its way.

To home-abiding women men will turn
From any stress, from any fresh disaster
(Seeking the faith and cheer for which men yearn;
Seeking a small room's shelter from the vaster
Ways of the world that tax their souls), and then
With strength renewed to fare them forth again.

The home-abiding women have the power
To link the world with God in its dark hour.

Soon Will the
Fluted Pools

Soon will the fluted pools
   Be quivering with rapture
Beneath the wind's kiss;
   And the heart will capture
The exquisite thrill
   Of the spring's returning,
And know again the quick,
   Sad, nostalgic yearning

For other springs long gone.
   The silvered wayside waters
Speak out with myriad tongues
   To earth's sons and daughters.
The elusive wind-flower's scent,
   The catkins heady swaying,
Can never say to hearts
   What the pools will soon be saying.

Cardinal in the Snow

Here he comes—a spurt of flame,
Red against unbroken white,
Here is beauty without name,
Here is color, fire and light.

His sharp whistle is as clear
As if summer wrapped him round:
A gay heartening thing to hear
When the snow is on the ground.

With no other life astir,
And the winter loathe to go,
There is nothing lovelier
Than a red bird in the snow.

Crab Tree in Bloom

How exquisite, how beautiful it is:
This crab tree filled with sun and radiant light.
I dare not look too long within its heart
Lest its bright, naked beauty blind me quite.

I shut my eyes and still the rosy cloud
Imprinted on closed lids is glimmering there;
My ears are brimming with the golden sound
The bees delight to loose upon the air.

A pink-white glory on a turquoise sky,
This tree upon an emerald hill in spring
Lays hold on me—I am not I at all,
But some tiptoe, ecstatic, breathless thing
Reaching to clasp a thousand petal tips,
To draw them down and press them to my lips.

April

April is a young girl
Coming through the meadow,
Her apron filled with wind-flowers,
Her eyes like silver stars,
Her step as light as thistledown,
Her lips as soft as feathers,
As I go out to meet her
Beside the pasture bars.

So young she is, so beautiful!
Her gown is pink and silver;
A mist is shining in her hair
Where swift the cool winds pass;
And suddenly before my eyes,
Wistful, sweet, and slender,
My own youth walks beside me
Across the meadow grass.

And swift as light another comes,
A young boy softly blowing
A whistle from a willow withe;
And sweet his tunes and high,
And all the years between are lost,
With my old heartache easing,
As young love draws me to his side
Beneath the April sky.

Fair Wind across the World

A fair wind blows across the world,
The morning light is bright as gold.
A million petals have unfurled—
For a power, too strong to hold,
Has opened up a darkened tomb
To set the Flower of Heaven free,
Piercing the long enshrouded gloom
For you and me.

Let us shield our eyes a moment here
Before the unaccustomed light.
It is so dazzlingly clear
After the troubled night.
And hearts, be still! the grief you bore,
In your long search for lasting peace,
Must be eased gradually before
This quick release.

We had forgotten all too long
The Easter time would come again
With hope and laughter, light and song
Along the ways of men.
We had forgotten . . . Oh, look up,
And hold high your long-emptied cup.

April Gardens

How fitting it was that April night,
To have brought Him back where a garden lay;
Cool and sweet in the early dusk
After a strange and terrible day.

How fitting that out of the dust of the years,
Up from a garden bed should rise
The white, the pure, the everlasting,
Beautiful flower of the skies.

How fitting that gardens everywhere
Recall Him today, His form, His face;
He walks there still in the evening light;
He moves through the morning's shadowy lace.

More radiant, far, than the first white flower,
Or the quivering light of a blossoming bough.
Deep in the gardens of any land,
Those who seek Him may find Him now.

The Gardener

Who breaks with fork and spade the stubborn sod,
Who hoes and rakes until each stubborn clod
Is powdered fine, works hand in hand with God.

For from him comes the rain and wind and sun,
The dewy nights when hot dry days are done,
To mellow well the work that has begun.

Who plants with careful hand the golden seed,
Who guards small tender shoots from thorn and weed,
Is a worker worthy of reward, indeed.

When up from dark rows, free of roots and rocks,
There leaps the flowering stems of hollyhocks,
And the light and joyous color of clumped phlox.

Worthy is he, when from his garden close,
There blooms the miracle men call a rose,
How well he has earned the rapture that he knows.

The Goodness of the Earth

Be glad for it—the goodness of the earth!
Rejoice in it—the splendid gift of God!
So much of beauty and so much of worth
Spring ever upward from the yielding sod.
All our possessions, table, bed, and chair,
Were uproots from the earth's full flowing breast,
Our roof, our daily bread, the clothes we wear
Spring from deep roots that mankind may be blest.

Let us rejoice, let us give grateful praise
For all good things that God has kept in store
Deep in the earth for need throughout our days.
God grant that as we use them more and more
They may be unexhausted, to bestow
Upon the generations yet to be
The earth's continued goodness, and the flow
Of life itself, which thine own hand sets free.

A Day's Value

Dawn, and noon, and night, then dawn again,
Flooding the earth with clear bright light that men
May take their straight, undeviating way
Along the glorious pathway of today
To high fulfillment, if they so desire.
There are ever hills to climb and lift them higher
Into the light and closer to the sky,
With the lodestar of the Word to steer them by;
There are the streams to ford, and valleys to be trod;
But the righteous pilgrim, hand-in-hand with God,
Makes headway straight and true to higher ground
Than any that he hitherto has found;
And there he goes, the light before his eyes
And hope within his heart. Ah, he is wise
Who counts the value of a day, then gives
His best to it each hour that he lives.

Birches in the Wind

Who, having once beheld this misty row
Of birches on a gusty April day,
Could ever leave them far behind and go
Unhindered down a drab and dusty way?
Surely the memory would leave its mark;
They are so cool, so exquisite, it seems
No one could quite forget their snowy bark
Or keep their leaves from tangling in his dreams.
Six white-barked birches on a windy hill—
When life is done they will be with me still.

Prayer
for
Common
Days

This is one of life's common days, dear Lord:
The same dull tasks await us, the same care
Lies heavily upon us with a weight
That often seems too great for hearts to bear.
And yet we know the day's tasks may become
Bright things of beauty, fraught with dignity,
And the heavy cares may suddenly grow light
When shared with thee.

Nothing is common. Help us keep in mind
The marvel of thy glorious gift of days.
Illuminate our minds that we may be
Conscious of thy presence, Lord. We praise
Thee hourly, daily, though our lot may seem
Circumscribed and limited and dull—
We are a part of thee, and all of life
Is beautiful.

Labor That Repays

Certain labor brings high pay
In a woman's life: the day
Fruit is gathered and preserved
Clear as amber, she has served
Well, indeed, and she can know
Satisfaction's ruddy glow.

When her wash is on the line,
And the snowy linens shine,
Mingled with gay prints that blow,
Whipped by wind, her heart can know
A glad partnership with the sun
And the wind, in work well done.

But the hour that best repays
In the silver coin of praise
Is the evening time when love
Holds her close, long mindful of
The high service she has given.
Truly, this is pay from Heaven.

Roses

In a rose's heart I see
The infinite love of God for me.
I marvel that he should trouble so
To make a twisted dark root grow

Until it lifts and shakes the air
With splendor. Oh, I am aware
That only God himself could bring
Out of the earth that gorgeous thing:

A yellow rose, its heart on fire
Like evening sunlight on a spire,
And only his great mind could think
Up this pale ecstasy, a pink

Pale rose where dawns have part
Within its lovely fragrant heart,
And, oh, a red rose . . . words I lack
To tell of velvet almost black,

Of a salmon rose with tips agleam
Like silver fishes in a stream.
Each is so beautiful! God knows
I love his gift of every rose.

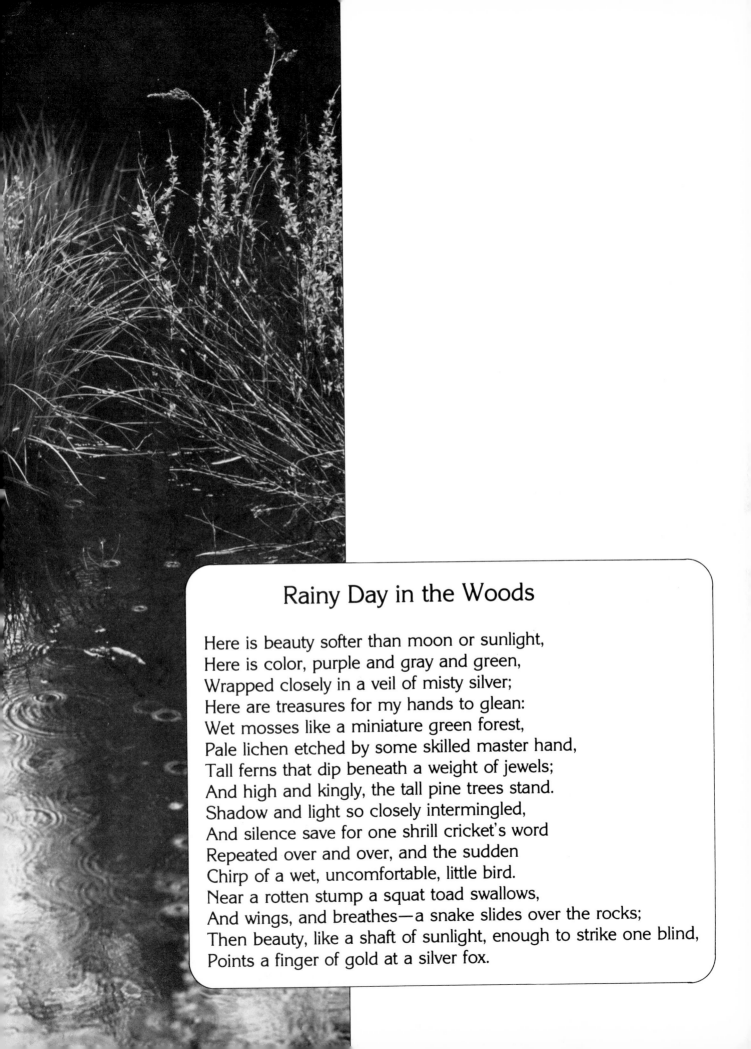

Rainy Day in the Woods

Here is beauty softer than moon or sunlight,
Here is color, purple and gray and green,
Wrapped closely in a veil of misty silver;
Here are treasures for my hands to glean:
Wet mosses like a miniature green forest,
Pale lichen etched by some skilled master hand,
Tall ferns that dip beneath a weight of jewels;
And high and kingly, the tall pine trees stand.
Shadow and light so closely intermingled,
And silence save for one shrill cricket's word
Repeated over and over, and the sudden
Chirp of a wet, uncomfortable, little bird.
Near a rotten stump a squat toad swallows,
And wings, and breathes—a snake slides over the rocks;
Then beauty, like a shaft of sunlight, enough to strike one blind,
Points a finger of gold at a silver fox.

Take Note of Beauty

"He hath made all things beautiful in His time!"
  Give heed to this, O hearts, for it will please
The great Creator of the world. Take note
  Of hill and valley, clouds, and brooks, and trees.

There is nothing He carelessly has made—
  Mark well the subtle intricacy of a flower
Deep-hidden in the wayside grass—formed there
  By an Artist's hand, to bloom for one brief hour.

Take note of beauty; God is mindful of
  His children's need for something to sustain
The heart throughout the clamor of our days.
  He sends the shine of sun, the silver rain;

He sets the light of dawn, the sunset fires
  Aglow for all who have the eyes to see.
Fail not, O hearts, to note His handiwork,
  His loving mindfulness of you and me.

Hospitality

Hospitality means not waiting
    For some invited guest
To sit beside one's table
    And partake of but the best.
It means the simple sharing—
    Perhaps of one's last crumb,
One's roof and cheerful fire
    With any who may come.

It matters not how humble
    A little home might be
When it is offered gladly
    Without apology;
When it is offered gaily
    As a gift that one would bring—
Hospitality thus given
    Is a lovely, gracious thing.

Home

Ah, he is blest indeed, who owns a home
    With raintight roof for shelter from the storm,
A table that is daily spread for him,
    And his own bright glowing fire to keep him warm.
And he is blest, who has a lighted lamp,
    A waiting chair, and a good book to read.
A few possessions are enough to meet
    The simple needs of men, when all is said.

Where these abide, and love is ever found,
    A selflessness, a bright coin, daily spent,
Four walls can be a haven here on earth;
    And there the heart can know a deep content.
God's greatest blessings on this earth's good loam,
    Are the dwelling places mankind calls home.

Neighbors

There is a closeness here that is closer than houses
   Set in a prim row on a quiet street;
There is a golden warmth more golden than sunshine,
   And a beautiful friendliness that is tender and sweet
One for another, when the need is greatest,
   Or when some heart is lit with a new delight,
And there is the willingness of proffered service
   That is given and accepted day or night.

"Nearby" is a word to fit these country neighbors,
   Nearby physically, and so very near
Spiritually in their understanding
   Of the hearts of one another . . . Oh, make clear
That there are neighbors still across the earth,
   Willing to share their table, roof and hearth.

Pity

They all have pitied me, my friends in town,
I wish that they could watch the sun go down
Beyond our hills; I wish that they might see
The crimson light tip every bush and tree;
Might see the green alfalfa churned to foam
By the late wind, and see the cows come home,
Bronzed in the sun! Oh, if they only knew
How peaceful and how beautiful the view
That lies beyond my wide clear windowpane,
They surely would not pity me again.

It has seemed odd to them to think that I,
Who live far out beneath this reach of sky,
Should pity them, but pity them I do.
They live too close for clean winds to blow through
Their cluttered lives; their houses, row on row,
Are as prim as the little potted plants that grow
Upon their windowsills. Bleak brick walls shut them in,
The smoky air is filled with fretting din;
They have no neighbors' friendly interchange:
I pity them . . . they laugh and think it strange!

The Plains

Even this land at last must yield to change:
The corrals and camps, the miles of open range,
The cattle on a thousand hills give place
To plows and tractors, and the steady pace
Known to the world as progress, but alas!
The round-up goes, the wild, wind-racing grass
Is broken into furrows, and the dense,
Round tumbleweeds lie still against a fence.

Only the vast still pastures of the sky
Remain unchanged. At night the herds go by,
Silvered with light. The whole run of the stars
Moving across it, with no hindering bars
To halt their wanderings . . . One all but hears
The tramp of hoofs, the bellowing of steers,
The "yip" of cowboys on those silvered heights . . .
Only of nights, only of starlit nights
Does this land we love seem changeless, only then
Is it wild and free and beautiful again.

Where have they gone, the horses that once trod
The roads of earth or tramped the pasture sod,
Nuzzling the grasses, where are they?   ## The Horses
Strange, indeed, that in so brief a day
There sounds down country lane or city street
No dusty plop-plop of their willing feet.

Strange that servants of mankind are gone
Beyond the sunset and beyond the dawn,
And leave no whinnying echo on the air.
The motors skim the concrete, but oh, where
Are the fringe-topped buggies and the manes that tossed
With pride of service? How much has been lost
Through progress, and gained no doubt, but oh,
The nostalgia for the far-off long ago!

Remove Not the Ancient Landmarks

Remove them not, the landmarks they have set.
Our founding fathers knew and talked with God.
Companioned thus, they never could forget
How sacred was this land. On clean, bright sod
They set their landmarks, staunch and firm and true;
They trusted us to keep them thus, but oh,
What have we done? And what will we yet do,
As onward through the hurrying years we go?
God stay our hands! May we cease to destroy
The marks that they have set: these last clear ones
That spell their faith, their honesty, their joy,
Their message to their daughters and their sons.
God help us that we may be mindful of
These ancient landmarks down the land we love.

Homes down the Land

These are the hope of any nation,
These are the gifts of God to man:
A home is his own divine creation,
His wise provision, his master plan.

With Christ as the head, the guest at the table,
With Christ in each room where a family lives,
Only thus will mankind be able
To pay the debt for the gift He gives.

He demands but little: the family altar,
Where strength is gathered for days ahead,
And life's small courtesies—why should we falter
In these to the Giver of roof and bread?

Its homes are a nation's vital power;
The Christian home is its strength and stay.
God, in this strange, bewildering hour,
Fortify every home, we pray.

That by Which We Live

It is not by bread alone by which we live;
It is not sight or touch or breath that keeps
The steady heartbeats pulsing in our breast;
Nor is it rest that comes to him who sleeps.
That by which we live is something more:
A vital and life-giving force that stays
Our heart, our hands, our feet—a force that gives
Us power to walk uprightly through our days.

Men call it faith—a substance yet unseen,
Impenetrable armor that we wear,
A shield held firm against the fiery darts
That evil may unloose upon the air.
It is a thing of splendor—a clear light
By which we travel safely day or night.

Faith

He who is strong in faith has riches
Beyond all wealth and beyond all price.
Light is the heart of him who travels
With faith on the highroad. Faith will suffice
To ease the way of the upward climbing,
And to help him over the lowland bogs.
Faith is a steady illumination,
A light that pierces the densest fogs.

O heart, whatever you lose, hold firmly
To faith, for better than wealth or fame
Is that possession—a priceless treasure,
Greater by far than earth's acclaim.
Faith is a rock, a sure foundation;
Faith is all things great and good;
Faith in God is our soul's foundation;
Let us hold fast to it as we should.

The Voice

We can hear God speak if we but listen;
We can hear His voice across the windblown grass;
We can hear Him speak from the far-off blue horizon,
And in the patience of the still rocks as we pass.
And deep down in the trusting eyes of children
Are tones as clear as any spoken word,
While in the good deeds men do for each other,
His insistent and approving voice is heard.

Within the glow of candlelight and fire
On any hearth at home, there comes the sound
Of benediction, drifting from the heavens,
Voicing His pleasure that His peace is found
Within the hearts and in the homes of mankind;
And, when at a crossroad, one must make a choice,
O hearts, stand still a little while and listen,
For the voice you hear will surely be His voice.

There is light and color in a field of wheat;
    And there is music rippling from the hand
Of God himself; and there is food to eat   Wheat
    Which lies like scattered manna on the land,
Each dripping golden globule is rife
    With the old eternal essences of life.

        And there are countless sickle blades ashine,
            With men to guide them down the fields of light;
        And there are mills to crush the golden grains fine,
            Then flour—leafy-brown, or snowy-white;
        And a million ovens everywhere that bake
            The wholesome daily bread for men to break.

But oh, the home-sweet loaves, the tended ones,
    That women through the centuries have made!
And offering to their husbands and their sons,
    The fragrant loaves that wait a sharp steel blade—
This bread of all the earth is the best:
    The bread, I feel, that must be doubly blest.

Bread

As old as life itself upon the earth
    Is the kneading and the baking of good bread;
As old as are the races, a red hearth
    Is a symbol of the need that man be fed.
Crude and coarse the ancient millings were
    With grain ground fine beneath two stones by one
Who performed the labor which belonged to her,
    And who felt a certain pride in work well done.

        One wonders not that Jesus often spoke
            Of bread—and that it played a vital part
        In his own daily living, that he broke
            It often for mankind, who broke his heart.
        "Take, eat," he said . . . as long as earth shall stand
            He will offer the bread of life with outstretched hand.

The First Apple Falls

There is a sudden stir in the orchard's grasses
As the first ripened apple falls to the ground.
Strange how softly footed the summer passes,
Strange that here in this place the only sound
Is that of an apple, loosed from its emerald moorings,
Seeking the earth as all must seek it at last:
The bud, the bloom, the green, the red fulfillment—
How quickly life is past!

I gather the apple, breathing its heady fragrance.
It is crisp and red; it is smooth and cool to my touch;
It is filled with goodness, as bread is to the hungry;
It is a gift of the gods to value much.
I feel I am the first to reap the fruitage
Of sun, and rain, and wind, and orchard tree,
As this first apple of a golden summer
Yields itself to me.

Alfalfa Harvest

Oh, beautiful and bright beyond all dreaming,
The alfalfa fields lie in the setting sun:
The greenest green on earth, a silver gleaming,
Sweeping them where the small winds dip and run.
And oh, the clean, cool, glorious sweetness of it!
I do not wonder that the birds sweep low,
And the butterflies and bees all love it,
And cling with small lips to it, loathe to go.
And now the harvesters have come to gather
Its emerald wealth, its prodigal green yield.
Their sickles echo through the autumn weather;
The wide swaths take it slowly, field by field.
And there the great rakes follow, dropping, lifting,
A glint of silver on each shifting tine,
And now with glinting forks the men are shifting
A fallen green that once was emerald wine.
Seasoned by sun and wind, at last 'tis ready
To bind in bales, that cattle might be fed;
But oh, my heart cannot forget the heady
Wine of the year that has been harvested.

The Feel of Autumn

There is a feel in the air today of autumn:
  Half sad, half glad, the wind goes on its way;
The first loosed leaf is scuttling down the pavement,
  The sky is gray.

Along the roadside blossoms the purple asters,
  The goldenrod are lamps set burning clear
Against the certain coming of a winter
  That will soon be here.

Strange how nostalgia clutches the heart in autumn
  And reiterates, in memory like a song,
The echo of beloved forgotten voices
  That have been stilled for long.

And as I walk across this windy meadow,
  My eyes grow dim with quick, unbidden tears . . .
There is the sound of footsteps walking beside me
  Of one who is gone for years.

The Roadway in September

The heat glimmers down on the long white road
  Where the latest strength of the sun is spent;
While out from each splash of shadow and shade
  The chill of the winter's breath is sent;

    Red, red are the berries of roses wild,
      And blue are the asters along the way,
    And down through the white of the thistle mist
      Gay butterflies dip in fantastic play.

        Oh, familiar the rustle of ripened corn
          And the sound of the pop of the milkweed pod;
        And sweet is the scent of the honeyed air
          From the field where the clover heads toss and nod;

          Deep in my heart is a tender thrill
            For the maiden and lover, who walk in the glow
          Of the September sun—as we used to walk,
            O lover of mine—in the long ago.

Here Is the Harvest

After the spring floods, after the drought,
After complainings from many a mouth,
Here is the harvest gathered in:
Granary and corncrib, barrel and bin,
Bursting with bounty from Thy hand,
Lord of our land!

We, Thy children, prone to doubt,
Prone in our plans to leave Thee out,
Turn, ashamed of our anxious fears,
Ashamed of our doubtings and our tears,
To thank Thee, Lord, for the great, good things
A harvest brings.

"Ye shall not sow your seed in vain,"
"There will be seedtime, there will be grain,"
Never a promise failing yet!
How, oh Lord, do our hearts forget?
Forgive us, God, and accept, we pray,
Our thanks today.

In the Golden Days

The crimson sumac rims the golden hills,
And in the valleys gleams the bundled grain;
All down the wooded way the blood-red glows
Where the queen Autumn's hectic cheek has lain;
And where her hand has touched the wild woodbine,
Its leaves are tipped with brilliant, scarlet stain.

Far in the distance yellow, burnished clouds
Of maple rain a golden shower bath;
All through the stubble glints the tender green
Of grass, the meadows freewill aftermath;
A whirling dust cloud hazes toward the sun
Where cattle straggle down a beaten path.

Down through its golden bars the great sun slips;
The still, brief twilight hastens, over-soon;
A faint flush heralds from the eastern hills
And lo! she comes, the glorious autumn moon.
She comes, and the sweet, radiant silver night
Supplants the mellow golden afternoon.

An Autumn Landscape

Brilliant scarlet and crimson stain,
And splashes of yellow gold,
Warm brown stubble and ripened grain,
The waysides seared and old,
A dazzle of green where the aftermath
Breathes a tale long told.

Gray where the haze hangs over the west,
Blue where the asters grow,
Purple the lights on a hill's far crest,
The shadows mauve below,
Blackbirds wheeling above the corn,
Silent, serenely slow.

Lights and shadows and sparkle of wine,
Somber color and gay,
Rich and warm in the late sunshine,
Chill where the shadows play,
Thus God hangs his masterpiece
Over the world today.

Cordwood

Piled goldenly within the winter wood
The ricks of cordwood stand; their even length
Beautifully straight, and strong, and good,
A testimony of earth's peculiar strength;
A testimony of inner working power:
The seed, the root, the trunk, the branch, the leaf,
The groping upward, slowly, hour by hour,
A long life, yet immeasurably brief.

Now, split and ready for some home-sweet hearth,
Its fragrance permeating the cold air,
It stands, neat-piled, a thing of vital worth,
Waiting the glittering axe, the hand to bear
It homeward; there to spend itself that men,
In from the cold, may warm themselves again.

Driftwood Fire

Summer is gone at last, and the wood I have gathered
Beside the sea, as a miser gathers his gold,
Lies on my grate, and lavishly now I am spending
A wealth that is far too great and precious to hold.
I strike a match, and a flame leaps up through the fagots
And runs like turbulent surf that seeks a shore;
Then wave after wave of brilliance springs into being
Where there was smouldering darkness a moment before.

The quick surprising transformations of color,
The restlessness of the flame, the splendor and light,
The ancient association of driftwood with ocean,
Makes me a wanderer upon far seas tonight.
The phosphorous-girdled islands are mine for the asking,
The dim, immeasurable waters of the earth
Have borne me away, an eager and willing captive,
Through the strange alchemy of sea-fire on my hearth.

A Woman Gives Thanks

Because the Lord has given me a home
And a good, kind man and a little plot of loam,
And I can plant a garden in the sun
Where flowers bloom and the winds of heaven run,
My heart goes singing on its joyous way,
And for God's goodness I give thanks today.
Our pilgrim mothers offered praise for these
Same gracious gifts; they thanked God on their knees
For simple things: for roof and fire and bed,
For homespun clothing and for daily bread.
Our need, as women, ever is the same
For shelter and a hearth fire's ruddy flame,
And for a God to worship and to praise
For his great goodness through the common days.
And on this special day, Lord God, I would
Join all mankind in sincere gratitude.

Fail Not to Thank the Giver

Fail not to thank the Giver of all good;
Fail not to thank him, though the year now past
Seems bleak and barren; let our gratitude
Lift high, because the darkness cannot last;
Because God's shining promises are rife
With hope for a fuller, more abundant life.

Fail not to thank him for each small, glad gift
That brightened hours that otherwise were dull:
The upward reach of trees, the joyous lift
Of wings against the wind, the beautiful,
Clear laughter of small children down the street,
The scent of garden flowers, fragrant, sweet.

Fail not to thank him for the gift of night
That brings the balm of peace when day is done;
Fail not to thank him for the steady light
Of courage, that the victory will be won;
And thank him humbly that his outstretched hand
Still showers his blessings on our own beloved land.

Christmas Eve on the Plains

I hold it true that men are nearer heaven
And closer by far to the never-failing stars,
Than mankind is in their overcrowded cities,
Out on these plains; there is nothing at all that bars
The waiting heart from the sky with its radiant splendor;
And nothing at all to distract the seeking mind.
I am so glad for this night with its silver silence;
I search and I find the thing that I came to find:

The peace that a burdened heart has so much need of,
The peace on earth that the Lord has meant for men.
Here alone in this vastness and the starlight
I shall live it over, that far-off night again,
When the angels sang their songs to the listening shepherds.
For I am a shepherd upon these plains tonight;
I shall turn and go with those others; I shall follow
The Light of the world, the Everlasting Light.

Christmas Eve at Home

Let us forget for a little while tonight
The clamor of the world, its wild unrest;
And let us set a candle with its light
Upon a sill; and know how very blest
Is any home, though humble it may be,
If Christ be worshiped, and if love be there,
In a Christian land where a people may be free
To live and labor, and to love and share.

O blest indeed, are they on Christmas Eve
Whose roofs are snug, whose fires are warmly red;
Where excited, eager children turn and leave
A room reluctantly, to go to bed;
And blest are they whose hands reach up to trim
Some small spruce tree whose branches soon will glow
With lovely light in memory of Him
Who came to light the whole world long ago.

So Many Things Are Lost

So many things are lost along the way:
Laughter, too often, and the silver light
Across the fields where little children play,
And bright, quick gladness . . . but, O heart, tonight
Let us be young for the little Christ Child's sake.
Let us again look out of youthful eyes
With the joyous thrill of one who lies awake,
Waiting for morning with its glad surprise.

The splendor still abides; the Christ is there.
The same road takes its followers to him.
The star still sheds its light upon the air.
God, God, the pity that our eyes grow dim,
And lose the glory. Help us, Lord, retrieve
The radiance of childhood's Christmas Eve.

This Is His Day

Out of the welter of the passing years,
　　This is His day—it should be set apart
To shine as a bright jewel shines through tears,
　　A precious gift to hold within the heart.

　　　　　　　Down through the centuries one radiant star
　　　　　　　　Still sheds its luminous lines of silver light.
　　　　　　　The time and distance cannot be too far,
　　　　　　　　And none need miss the way across the night.

　　This is His night—His day. His call for peace
　　　Is sounding out like a clear trumpet blast.
　　His plea for all to heed will never cease
　　　Till nations move in unity at last.

　　　　　　Surely the goodwill that He bade us keep
　　　　　　　Toward all mankind will bear its golden fruit.
　　　　　　God help us gather it . . . God help us reap
　　　　　　　The good grain springing up from that deep root.

Christmas Today

Into this strange wilderness we call "today,"
　　May a million chimes peal out upon the air;
May the countless voices of earth's choirs lift
　　To cry aloud the good news everywhere:
That unto us this night the Christ is born,
　　The same Christ of that far night of birth,
Who left the ivory palaces of heaven
　　To tread the roughened roadways of the earth.

Let the men of the fields and those of the cities come;
　　Let pauper and royalty journey from near and far,
Linked in a unison of brotherly love
　　That is welded together by one white molten star,
To find the Christ that many have lost for long,
　　O chimes ring out, O voices lift your song!

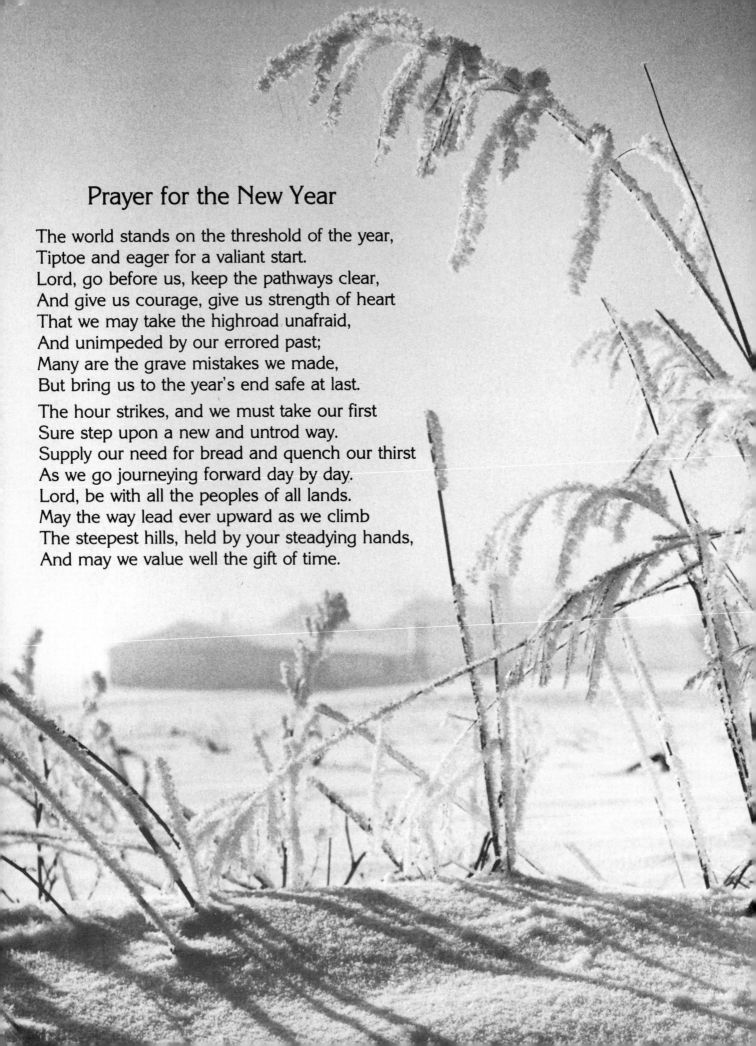

Prayer for the New Year

The world stands on the threshold of the year,
Tiptoe and eager for a valiant start.
Lord, go before us, keep the pathways clear,
And give us courage, give us strength of heart
That we may take the highroad unafraid,
And unimpeded by our errored past;
Many are the grave mistakes we made,
But bring us to the year's end safe at last.

The hour strikes, and we must take our first
Sure step upon a new and untrod way.
Supply our need for bread and quench our thirst
As we go journeying forward day by day.
Lord, be with all the peoples of all lands.
May the way lead ever upward as we climb
The steepest hills, held by your steadying hands,
And may we value well the gift of time.